A RIVER JOURNEY

The
Amazon

Simon Scoones

HODDER
Wayland

an imprint of Hodder Children's Books

A RIVER JOURNEY

The Amazon	The Ganges
The Mississippi	The Nile
The Rhine	The Yangtze

A *River Journey*: *The Amazon*
Copyright © 2003 Hodder Wayland
First published in 2003 by Hodder Wayland,
an imprint of Hodder Children's Books.

Commissioning Editor: Victoria Brooker   Cover design: Hodder Wayland   Book design: Jane Hawkins
Book Editor: Belinda Hollyer   Picture Research: Shelley Noronha, Glass Onion Pictures
Book consultant: Duncan McGregor, Senior Lecturer in Geography, University of London   Maps: Tony Fleetwood
The author would like to thank Alex Shankland and Jose Assuncão for their help.
Series consultant: Rob Bowden, EASI-Educational Resourcing

Series concept by: Environment and Society International –
                        Educational Resourcing

British Library Cataloguing in Publication Data
Scoones, Simon
  Amazon. - (A river journey)
  1.Amazon River - Juvenile literature 2.Amazon River -
  Geography - Juvenile literature
  I.Title
  918.1'1

07502 40326

Printed in Hong Kong

Hodder Children's Books
A division of Hodder Headline Ltd
338 Euston Road, London NW1 3BH

Picture Acknowledgements
Cover Dr Morley Read/Science Photo Library; title page Michel Roggo/Still Pictures; 2 Edward Parker/Still Pictures; 5 Jane Hawkins; 6 Simon Scoones; 7 Simon Scoones; 8 top Simon Scoones, below Panos/A. Bungeroth; 9 South American Pictures/Tony Morrison, inset Art Wolfe/Science Photo Library; 10 Simon Scoones, inset Richard Packwood/Oxford Scientific Films; 11 Tony Morrison/South American Pictures; 12 Tony Morrison/South American Pictures; 13 left Tony Morrison/South American Pictures, right South American Pictures; 14 Tony Morrison/South American Pictures, Simon Scoones; 15 Hart/Reflejo; 16 Dr Morley Read/Science Photo Library; 17 left Sinclair Stammers/Science Photo Library, right Partridge Films Ltd/Oxford Scientific Films; 18 Fred Hoogervorst/Panos; 19 Arabella Cecil/Panos; 20 Julia Waterlow/Eye Ubiquitous; 21 left Edward Parker/Still Pictures, right Sue Cunningham/ SCP; 22 Simon Scoones; 23 top Edward Parker/Still Pictures, bottom Gregory Ochocki/Science Photo Library; 24 top Douglas Faulkner/Science Photo Library, bottom Kevin Schafer/Still Pictures; 25 Steve Bowles/ South American Pictures, bottom K. Gillham/Robert Harding; 26 Tony Morrison/South American Pictures; 27 top Edward Parker/Still Pictures, right Simon Scoones; 28 Robert Harding; 29 Mark Edwards/Still Pictures, inset Edward Parker/ South American Pictures; 30 Ken Gillham/Robert Harding; 31 Jean Chrisstophe Vie/Still Pictures; 32 K. Gillham/ Robert Harding, inset Simon Scoones; 33 Sue Cunningham/SCP, bottom Karen Ward/South American Pictures; 34 Ken Gillham/Robert Harding; 35 Tony Morrison/South American Pictures; 36 Jevan Berrange, inset Hellier Mason/Still Pictures; 38 Nigel Dickinson/Still Pictures; 39 top Geospace/Science Photo Library, inset Herbert Giradet/Still Pictures, bottom Topham Picture Point; 40 Martin Wendler/Still Pictures; 41 Sue Cunningham/ SCP; 42 left Jacques Jangoux/Science Photo Library, right Tony Allen/Oxford Scientific Films; 43 Tony Morrison/ South American Pictures; 44 Ken Gillham/Robert Harding; 45 left Mark Edwards/Still Pictures, right NASA/Still Pictures

Contents

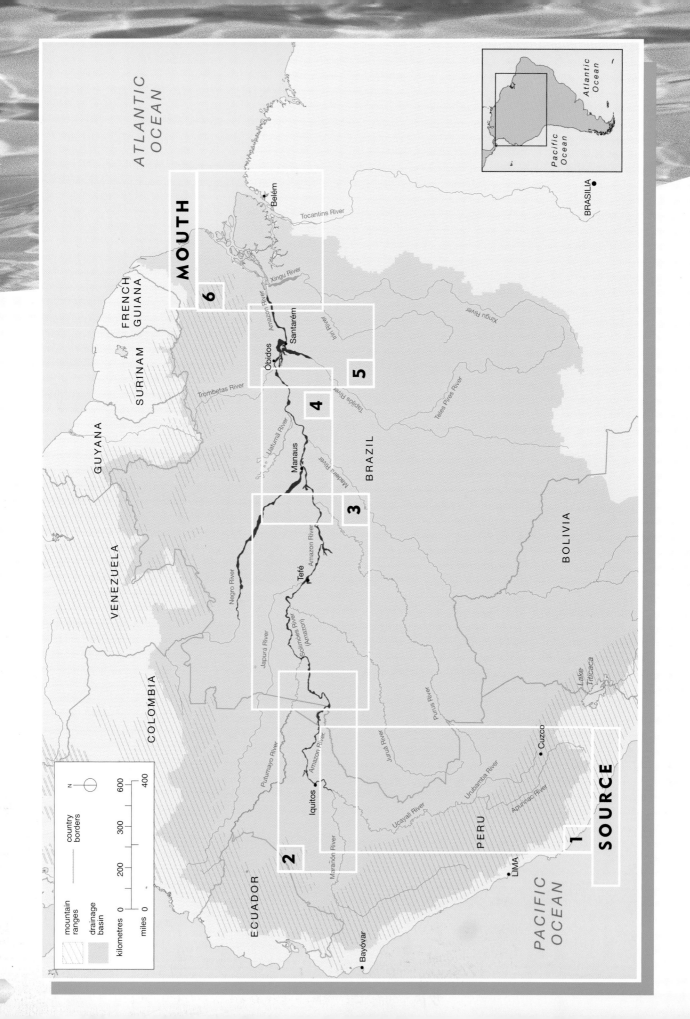

ATLANTIC OCEAN

Atlantic Ocean

BRASÍLIA

Pacific Ocean

MOUTH

FRENCH GUIANA

Belém

Tocantins River

SURINAM

6

Xingu River

Amazon River

Santarém

Iri River

Xingu River

Óbidos

5

Trombetas River

Tapajós River

GUYANA

Teles Pires River

Uatumã River

4

Manaus

BRAZIL

Madeira River

3

VENEZUELA

Negro River

Tefé

Amazon River

BOLIVIA

Japurá River

Solimões River (Amazon)

Lake Titicaca

COLOMBIA

Putumayo River

Purus River

Cuzco

Juruá River

2

Amazon River

SOURCE

Iquitos

Ucayali River

Urubamba River

Apurímac River

Marañón River

PERU

1

ECUADOR

LIMA

Bayóvar

PACIFIC OCEAN

mountain ranges

country borders

drainage basin

N

kilometres 0   200   300   600
miles   0   400

Your Guide to the River

USING THEMED TEXT As you make your journey down the Amazon you will find topic headings about that area of the river. These symbols show what the text is about.

🐰 **NATURE** Plants, wildlife and the environment

📖 **HISTORY** Events and people in the past

✋ **PEOPLE** The lives and culture of local people

➡️ **CHANGE** Things that have altered the area

$ **ECONOMY** Jobs and industry in the area

USING MAP REFERENCES Each chapter has a map that shows the section of the river we are visiting. The numbered boxes show exactly where a place of interest is located.

PERU

Purus River

Cuzco •

km 0   200

miles 0   200

The Journey Ahead

Our journey begins in Peru, high up in the Andes Mountains. Here, the Urubamba River, one of the Amazon's tributaries, is born. From there we head north, following the river as it gushes down the mountain slopes into a huge low-lying region. Then the Amazon River winds its way through the world's largest area of tropical rainforest. This is one of the few places left on Earth where plants and animals have yet to be discovered. Beyond the city of Iquitos the Amazon River makes a sharp turn east, following the equator, and enters the country of Brazil. Finally, we reach the Atlantic coast, nearly three thousand kilometres away. Here, where the Amazon spills into the ocean, the river is so wide you cannot see across to the other bank.

We begin our journey in the snowy peaks of the Andes. Get your hiking boots on, and wrap up warm!

1. A *river with many beginnings*

IT IS HARD TO SAY EXACTLY where the Amazon River begins, because it is fed by so many other rivers. It probably begins in the 'altiplano' (the high plains) of the Andes Mountains. Here, the land collects the melted ice and rainwater that flow off the high peaks. These marshy areas form the Urubamba River, one of the Amazon's tributaries.

Below: The ancient city of Machu Picchu is one of the wonders of the world. It takes four days to walk here along an Inca trail, but many tourists take a train ride instead.

Nauta

Marañon River

Juruá River

BRAZIL

Ucayali River

Urubamba River

Purus River

PERU

1

Cuzco

km 0   200

miles 0   120

Above: The Incas were skilled architects and engineers. Many of their stone walls still stand.
Right: The Urubamba River is joined by thousands of tiny mountain streams. It has enough force to cut a path through valleys, like this one, in the Andes Mountains.

📖 HISTORY A *sacred valley*

The Urubamba river valley is known as the sacred valley of the Incas. The Incas were a people that settled here about 800 years ago. The valley became their storehouse for food.

The Incas developed farming techniques to cope with the steep mountain environment. By cutting into the slopes, they created terraced fields that look like giant steps in the mountains. The Incas watered their fields by draining water from the Urubamba River, through channels carved from the rock. Some channels flowed through their streets, and brought water to their homes.

The Incas had one of the world's most sophisticated ancient civilisations. The vast Inca empire was dotted with majestic cities that were linked by stone-paved roads, steps and pathways across the mountains and beyond. The Incas could easily travel from place to place, trading food and other goods.

But the Inca empire was conquered by the Spanish in the 1500s, and their civilisation was destroyed.

💲 ECONOMY *Machu Picchu tourists*

Today, thousands of tourists flock to the Urubamba valley each year to marvel at the ancient city of Machu Picchu MAP REF: 1. Machu Picchu is perched on a narrow ridge, 300 metres above the Urubamba River. The city remained hidden for five hundred years, until an American archaeologist called Hiram Bingham visited the area in 1911. After a tip-off from a local farmer, Hiram Bingham crawled up steep slopes and fought his way through thick jungle vines and trees, until he found the ruins.

Above: The terraces of Moray are hidden in the depths of the Incas' sacred valley. Here, the Incas tried out new crops. The person in the middle shows you how enormous the terraces are.

Left: A young Quechua girl with an alpaca. Her hat and shawl are made from alpaca wool.

$ ECONOMY *Potatoes, llamas & alpacas*

The local people in this region are named after the Inca language they speak, called Quechua. Many Quechua people are descendants of the Incas. Like the Incas before them, the Quechua depend on the Urubamba River and the fertile silt it leaves behind. They learned from their ancestors how to farm the land without damaging it. By mixing crops together, or by changing crops from year to year, Quechua farmers keep a balance of nutrients in the soil. Quechua communities also care for each other, and help their neighbours, just as the Incas did.

The Quechua grow more than 400 different types of potato, and rear herds of llama and alpaca. Llamas are strong, and can transport goods that are too heavy for people to carry. The Quechua also eat llama meat. The llama's woolly cousin, the alpaca, is also a very useful animal. The Quechua weave alpaca wool into warm garments and turn alpaca hides into coats, to keep them warm through the worst of the cold Andean winter.

It is very difficult to make a living in this harsh environment. Some Quechua farmers have abandoned their land. They have moved down into towns in the Urubamba valley, where they sell goods to tourists.

 NATURE *A blanket of cloud*

The mountain slopes high above the Urubamba River can receive six metres of rainfall in a year. These slopes are often covered in a blanket of water vapour. In such a damp, misty environment, a belt of cloud forest sucks water from the clouds, acting like a huge sponge. The water is released slowly, dripping off the trees and plants. Because the process is so slow, floods or landslides from too much water in the valley below seldom happen.

Walking into a 'cloud forest' is like entering a magical kingdom in every shade of green. With all the water around, plants

Above: Plants that live on other plants, like ferns, orchids and bromeliads, are called epiphyte or guest plants. The red bird is a Cock-of-the-Rock.

cling to every branch and tree trunk, and create a hanging garden. In the cloud forest you can find more types of plant in a small area than in the whole of Europe. Many are found nowhere else. The cloud forest has its own special animals and birds too, such as the many kinds of frog that live in the undergrowth, or in pools of water on the ground.

If we are really lucky, we might see the flame-red Cock-of-the-Rock bird, performing its mating dance in the early morning mist.

Fast & furious water

The Urubamba River twists and turns through mountain gorges, until it turns north. Then the river and its tributaries slide down the high mountains into the foothills of the Andes. When it leaves the mountains, the Urubamba changes its name to the Ucayali River. The dramatic fall in elevation gives the river extra energy. It flows fast and furiously, eroding its bed and banks, and carrying rocks, soil, leaves and branches downstream. Wild, foaming rapids form on the river's surface, as it crashes into boulders that block its path. These boulders provide perfect perches for kingfishers and herons. They can hunt for fish in the river's turbulent currents.

The change in altitude brings warmth, and more rain. As the water on the ground warms up, it evaporates, rises, and turns into water vapour. Torrential tropical downpours can follow when there is so much moisture in the air. With the change in climate, tropical rainforest replaces the cloud forest in these hot, sticky lowlands.

Right: A kingfisher waits for a fish in the waters of the Urubamba River.
Below: Rapids form on the surface of the river as the water crashes around the rocks.

Indians of the **Amazon**

American Indians (known as AmerIndians) have lived in these tropical rainforests for 15,000 years. During the last Ice Age, their ancestors moved across to the Americas from central Asia. When the first Europeans explored the Amazon basin in the sixteenth century, about two million AmerIndians lived in different parts of the forest.

Today, however, there are probably only 250,000 AmerIndians left in the Amazon basin. Some were killed by the Europeans who took over large areas. Many more were forced into slavery, or died from diseases like measles that were caught from the European settlers.

During our journey, we will meet and learn more about the Indians. Each AmerIndian group has developed its own way of life over generations. Some live together in settled villages. Others are nomads, and move every few days in search of food in the forest or the river. At least fifty groups have had no contact with the outside world. They still live as they have done for hundreds of years.

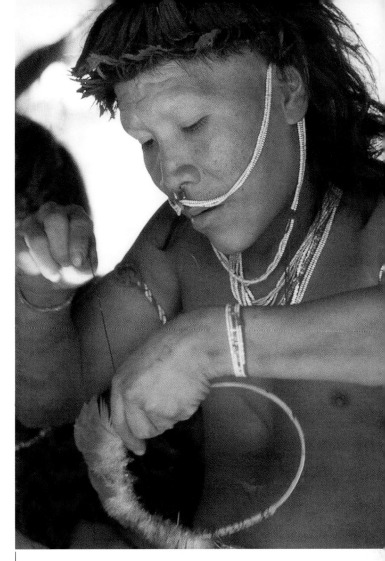

Above: This AmerIndian is a member of a group in Peru. In that country AmerIndians have the right to own land, unlike their neighbours in Brazil.

 NATURE *The real* **Amazon**

Near the town of Nauta, in eastern Peru, an important event happens. The Ucayali River, on which we are travelling, is joined by the Marañón River. The Marañón also began its journey in the Andes mountains. It has come 1,800 kilometres to this point - one and half times further than the entire length of the Rhine, which is the longest river in western Europe. Now the Marañón River joins the Ucayali, and one vast channel of water is formed. From here onwards, our river is called the Amazon.

AmerIndians build log rafts, bound up by liana vines. Let's take one of these rafts and head north through the tropical rainforest - don't forget your paddle!

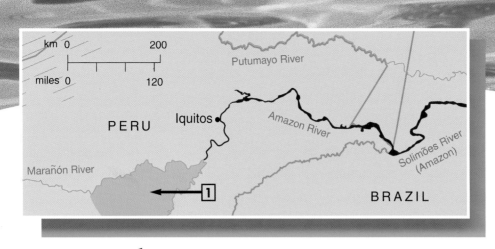

2. Towards the three-way frontier

MANY SMALLER RIVERS JOIN THE AMAZON in the lowlands of Peru. Some of these begin in Colombia in the north, and in Ecuador to the west. The Amazon River is now very flat, but the flow is still powerful because there is so much water pouring off the mountains. With all that energy, the Amazon wears away its bed and banks. Its channel is deep and wide by the time we reach the city of Iquitos.

Below: The Amazon wears away the outside of its channel, and deposits silt on the inside. That is why the river bends - or meanders - into the snaking shapes you see here.

Above left: The Yagua people live near the city of Iquitos. Since the first Europeans arrived, the Yagua refused to speak Spanish, and have kept their own language and system of beliefs. They are one of many AmerIndian groups who still seek advice and help from their own priests, called shamans.

Above right: When the Spanish missionaries came to South America, they tried to make AmerIndians become Christians. This old engraving shows a Spanish priest explaining his religion to AmerIndians in a church. The people do not look very interested in what he is saying!

📖 HISTORY *Explorers & missionaries*

Francisco de Orellana was the first European to reach this stretch of the Amazon, when he travelled from Ecuador to the Atlantic coast in 1541. He was surprised to see great settlements of Indians living by the river. Like many Europeans of the time, Francisco de Orellana thought AmerIndians were primitive. He believed they needed to be 'civilised' by European ideas and traditions. But in fact, the AmerIndians were very intelligent, with many skills. Orellana did not know the proud history of many AmerIndian groups, or their detailed understanding of their environment.

Later, Catholic missionaries came from Europe to convert AmerIndians to Christianity. The missionaries tried to learn AmerIndian languages, so they could explain their faith more easily. But AmerIndians had their own belief systems. Their gods were connected to the river, the trees, the earth, the sun and the moon. They resisted Catholic beliefs, and killed many missionaries with their poison dart blowpipes.

No roads to Iquitos

Iquitos, on the banks of the Amazon, is a city with 400,000 inhabitants. It is also the largest city in the world that cannot be reached by road. The only way to get to Iquitos is by boat along the river, or by air. There are almost no cars in Iquitos, because there are no roads to bring them in. Instead, bicycles and three-seater motor carts fill the streets. Ferries, called collectivos, take people and goods across the river. And, because of the Amazon's deep, wide channel, boats can take passengers from Iquitos all the way to the Atlantic coast, 3,700 kilometres away.

The centre of Iquitos bustles with activity. People trade goods amongst themselves, and with people from outlying villages. Markets on the banks of the river sell fruit and vegetables, fish, tobacco and timber. At the food stalls you could buy a local delicacy - like turtle meat soup, or fried or steamed monkey! Or you could try palmeta, a local soup made from river fish.

Left: Pedal power is very important in a town without cars, like Iquitos.
Below: These cashews on sale in Iquitos market have several uses. The outer flesh, called the apple, can be squeezed to make delicious juice. And the nut in the middle makes a delicious snack, either raw or roasted.

Above: These houses have been built along the river bank in Iquitos. The photograph was taken in the dry season - imagine how this looks in the rainy season, when the river level has risen.

PEOPLE *Living with the river*

The people of Iquitos have to cope with changing water levels in different seasons, because they live so close to the river. Thousands of people make their homes on the edge of the city, where they build houses from whatever materials they can find, such as bamboo and corrugated iron. But this land floods every year when the river rises. People here must switch from bicycles to canoes to get around.

To keep dry, many people build their houses on stilts. Other houses are built on balsa wood logs. Balsa wood is very light, and floats easily. That means the houses can float when the river level rises.

$ ECONOMY *The oil business*

Iquitos is the centre for exploring the oil and natural gas reserves that lie beneath the rock, in this part of the Amazon basin. The Amazon's oil has become big business. Nearly a quarter of all the oil that the United States of America imports, comes from here. Once the oil is pumped from the ground it is either sent by pipeline, or taken by barge, along the river to the Loreto oil refinery, near Iquitos. Then the crude oil is heated and separated into different parts, such as benzine, kerosene and gasoline.

Refined oil from this part of the Amazon basin is now pumped through the Norperuano pipeline. This is Peru's longest pipeline and stretches for 800 kilometres. It goes right over the Andes, all the way west to the port of Bayóvar on the Pacific Ocean.

→ CHANGE *The impact of oil*

Oil has improved the lives of many people in the Amazon basin by bringing jobs and wealth to the area. But it has also brought new risks and problems. In October 2000, 5,500 barrels of oil were spilled into the Marañón River. The river water was polluted over a vast area. Some of the leaked oil spread into the nearby Pacaya Samiria Reserve MAP REF: 1 , Peru's largest protected area, where it caused enormous damage.

For the 20,000 people that depend on the river's water, the effects of the oil spill have been devastating. Fish catches are tiny in comparison to the size they were before the spill, because so many fish were poisoned or suffocated by the oil. This has deprived local people of their main food source. Many AmerIndians have developed skin diseases and stomach infections, from drinking or washing in the polluted water.

✋ PEOPLE *The Urarina people*

The Urarina are a shy and peaceful group of Indians, who have lived around the Marañón River for hundreds of years. Now their livelihood is threatened by outsiders who are moving into their homeland.

Hidden in this swampy area of forest, the Urarina clear small gardens to plant crops like manioc, corn and banana. They fish in the river, and are experts at using blowpipes

Left & below: The Amazon basin when oil is discovered. The dark square on the left is an abandoned oil well. The forest below has been cleared to make room for a settlement, and an oil pipeline runs across the burned tree stumps.

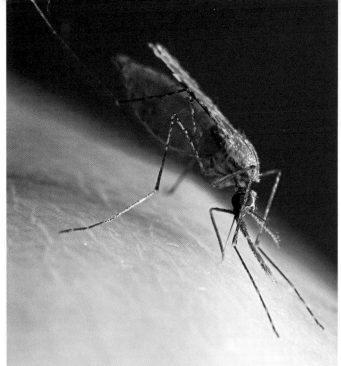

Above: A female anopheles mosquito spreads the malaria parasite in its saliva. The parasite can be transferred to humans if the mosquito bites them.
Right: Poachers in the Urarina lands hunt and kill saki monkeys for their beautiful tails. The tails are then sold as dusters.

to hunt animals. But oil companies searching for oil, logging companies cutting down trees, and even tourists in search of a different experience, have all come in contact with the Urarina.

Because they are not used to outside contact, the Urarina do not have any natural protection from outside diseases. This means they are at greater risk of getting ill from contact with new people. The results can be devastating. In recent years, many Urarina people have caught deadly diseases such as malaria and cholera. Diseases like these could threaten their very existence.

Poachers are also a serious problem. They sneak on to Urarina land to catch local monkeys called 'monk saki'. But the Urarina have formed their own protection squads, called the 'river wolves'. Divided into teams of four, the river wolves take turns to guard their territory against poachers. They also watch the river, and try to stop poachers using poison to catch fish. Poison can kill the wildlife in whole sections of the river.

Let's ride in a dug-out canoe to the three-way frontier of Peru, Colombia and Brazil. From there, we will cross the border into Brazil.

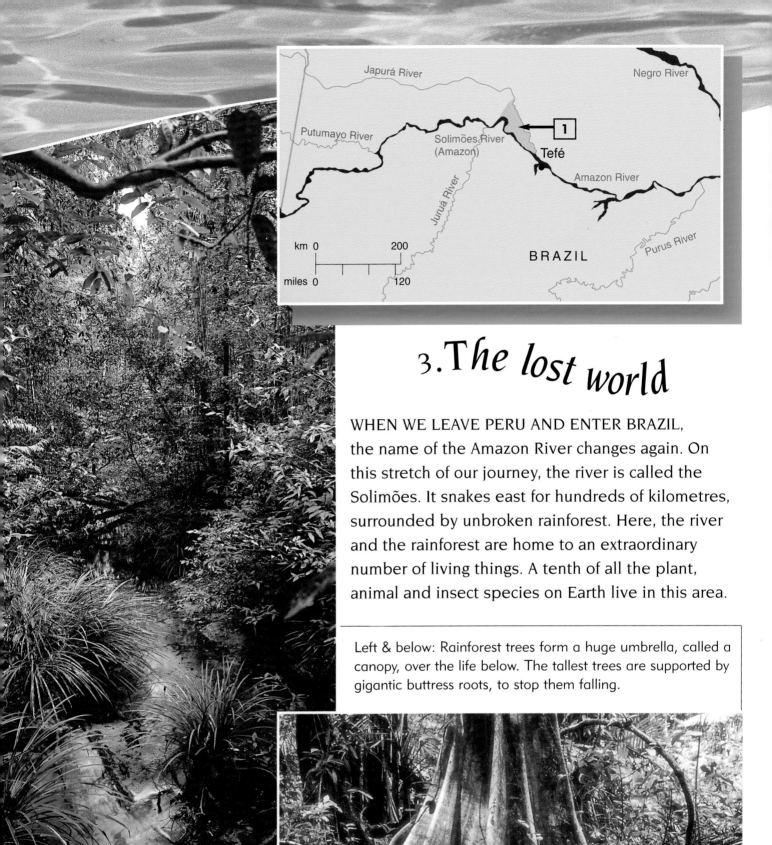

Japurá River

Negro River

Putumayo River

Solimões River
(Amazon)

1

Tefé

Amazon River

Juruá River

km 0   200

BRAZIL

Purus River

miles 0   120

3. The lost world

WHEN WE LEAVE PERU AND ENTER BRAZIL,
the name of the Amazon River changes again. On
this stretch of our journey, the river is called the
Solimões. It snakes east for hundreds of kilometres,
surrounded by unbroken rainforest. Here, the river
and the rainforest are home to an extraordinary
number of living things. A tenth of all the plant,
animal and insect species on Earth live in this area.

Left & below: Rainforest trees form a huge umbrella, called a
canopy, over the life below. The tallest trees are supported by
gigantic buttress roots, to stop them falling.

NATURE *The rainforest cycle of life*

All the world's rainforests are close to the Equator. Rainforest trees and plants can grow every day of the year, because of the abundant rain, sunshine and hot temperatures. The hot, wet conditions also speed up the rate at which dead leaves and branches decompose on the forest floor. Many types of fungi help to break down this rotting material, and then the nutrients they contain can be used again. A network of tree roots on the forest floor sucks up some of these nutrients before they are washed away by the rain, or seep into the underlying soil.

By recycling the nutrients, rainforest trees grow to amazing heights. The tallest trees, like the kapok, can be forty metres high. To stop them falling, the trees are supported by gigantic buttress roots. Other plants and vines grow along the branches of these forest giants. The trees also provide food and habitats for animals and birds. Some trees have leaves with special drip tips, which shield the land from tropical downpours. In this way, the trees create

Above: A scarlet macaw flies over a patch of Victoria Regia lilies. The lilies were named by a British naturalist in the nineteenth century, after Queen Victoria. These lily pads can grow up to two metres in diameter.

a vast umbrella which protects the human, plant and animal life of the forest.

Rainwater drains into the river from the surrounding forest. It carries some of the nutrients in soil particles, or dissolved in the water that was not absorbed by tree roots. These nutrients provide food for an abundance of life in the river itself.

Scientists guess that there may be three thousand types of fish in the river. New species are being found all the time. The murky depths of the river are home to many strange life forms, like transparent catfish, and electric fish that hunt without sight and live off the tails of other electric fish.

Where the water is calm, Victoria Regia lilies grow across the surface of the river. Spikes underneath the pads keep away nibbling fish. The lily pads provide a useful platform for nimble-footed birds that search for insects on the water's surface.

PEOPLE Living *in the* rainforest

In order to survive in the rainforest, the AmerIndians have developed a deep understanding of it. They have learned that the soil loses its fertility if they plant crops year after year. To give the soil a chance to recover, they move on to a new patch of forest.

AmerIndians also know that cutting down trees cuts off the supply of nutrients to the soil. So they use the forest resources without cutting down trees. The sap from one tree makes a firelighter, and another tree's bark makes very strong rope. Hitting the hollow trunks of the drum tree is an excellent way to send messages echoing through the forest. The AmerIndians also use some plants to decorate themselves,

making vivid dyes from seeds, bark and leaves. They even use some soft, spongy leaves as toilet paper.

Whether they are visiting a friend or a neighbour, or even going to school, most people on this stretch of the river travel by canoe. AmerIndians can make a canoe from a single tree trunk. At times of conflict in the past, some Indian groups carved canoes big enough for thirty warriors out of just one of the forest giants. To make sure they last for years, the people fill their canoes with water when they are not in use. That stops the wood from drying out and splitting. In their canoes, AmerIndians hunt

Left: An AmerIndian boy paddles his canoe on the Amazon River.
Above: A small pirarucu is caught. Pirarucu fish can be up to four metres long, and may weigh as much as a cow!
Right: This AmerIndian child's skin is painted with vegetable dye patterns. The red dye on his face is made from curucum seeds.

fish like the pirarucu, the world's largest freshwater fish.

Indians also use the rainforest to make music. They carve a kind of flute from a piece of bamboo, or the hollow leg bone of an animal. Gourds also make good instruments. Gourds are made from the dried and hollowed skin of fruits such as pumpkin and squash. The gourds are filled with seeds or stones from the riverbank, to make a percussion instrument known as a maraca. The shuffling sound of maracas is heard at parties and festivals all over Brazil.

To protect the land used by different groups of AmerIndians, there are now twenty-nine Indian reserves in the Amazon basin. This helps to protect forest traditions and knowledge, so the people can pass on their expertise to future generations.

NATURE *Rising waters*

Although rain showers happen all year in the Amazon basin, most rain falls between January and March. During this wet season, rainwater pours off the land and surges down the tributaries into the main river channel. The swollen river rises twenty metres, and floods an area the size of England. In this season the Amazon holds more water than the next eight largest rivers on Earth, all put together.

The water level spills over the land and rises in the igapos - the parts of the forest that are permanently flooded. But the river floods other parts of the forest too. That creates a maze of seasonal islands and extra water channels. In the flooded forest, insects fall from the treetops and provide food for fish. Fish such as the fruit-eating tambaqui help to disperse seeds. They eat the fleshy outsides, and the seeds pass straight through the fish. The seeds end up somewhere else in the water. Meanwhile, predators such as caiman, members of the alligator family, hunt their prey amongst the reeds.

In the rainforest canopy, groups of monkeys jump from tree to tree, feeding on leaves and fruits. The white uacari monkey lives only in the flooded forest, eating the seeds of unripe fruits. These agile animals can leap up to thirty metres from one tree to another. They have no fur on their heads at all, and their faces are bright red. Sloths are not so athletic. But to move around the flooded forest in search of their next meal, sloths have had to learn how to swim.

By October, the tropical downpours are less frequent and less heavy. During this relatively dry season, the river level drops, and the much of the flooded forest is dry land once again. Some channels of water become completely cut off, forming small lakes in the forest.

A myth surrounds the pink dolphin, another resident of the flooded forest. These beautiful creatures, called bôto, feed off small fish in the igapos. They are the only dolphins that can bend their necks.

During the Feast of St. John every June, people gather to eat, dance and have a good time. The bôto is supposed to visit the party. He comes disguised as a handsome young man, but he has to wear a hat to hide the nostrils on top of his head.

The bôto dances with the first beautiful woman he meets, persuading her to come with him to the bottom of the river. It is traditional to ask any man who is wearing a hat to take it off, to check that there is no bôto amongst the guests!

Left: A uacari monkey. Local people say that the red faces of these monkeys remind them of the sunburned faces of Europeans.
Below: The bôto - the pink dolphin - is almost blind. It uses sonar to find its way through the murky waters of the Amazon River.

Above: Manatees are gentle and inquisitive animals. Some people think that the myth of mermaids is based on sightings of manatees.
Left: Scarlet macaws sometimes eat wet clay from the river bank. No one knows exactly why, but the clay may help settle their stomachs after a meal of sour fruits and berries.

NATURE *The Mamiraua*

The Japurá River joins the Solimões River near the town of Tefé. A reserve called Mamiraua MAP REF: 1 sits in the watery triangle between the two rivers. During the wet season, the water here rises twelve metres, making it the largest protected area of flooded forest in Brazil. 'Mamiraua' is an AmerIndian word for a baby manatee. Manatees are one of the many rare animals that live here. They can grow up to three metres long, and have seal-like bodies with powerful flat tails.

The Mamiraua Reserve helps to protect some of the world's endangered species. It also gives scientists a chance to learn more about them. Eighty researchers are based here, to study the flooded environment.

But Mamiraua is different from other reserves in an important way. Instead of banning local people from using the area, their needs are taken into account. Some parts of the reserve are strictly protected, but the five thousand people who live here can fish, and collect wood, in other parts. Local people help manage the reserve. So the lives of the people and the wildlife of Mamiraua can both be maintained.

$ ECONOMY *Medicines & poisons*

Scientists already know that some rainforest plants have medicinal qualities. These qualities have helped cure illnesses for centuries. The bark of one tree contains quinine, one of the oldest cures for malaria. The study of rainforest plants continues, in the hope of finding cures for other illnesses.

AmerIndians have always used the forest for different medicines. They collect a nut called guaraná, known as the 'red gold' of the Amazon. Nowadays, guaraná is often ground into a powder and mixed with milk. Drinking one of these guaraná milkshakes will give you extra energy. AmerIndians have introduced us to different foods, too. The cacao is a tall rainforest tree. It produces large red fruitpods that contain the main ingredient in chocolate.

Above: A scientist in the Mamiraua Reserve collects samples of rainforest plants.

Not all Amazonian plants are used to heal or nourish. One plant called curare is used as a poison. If a monkey high in the rainforest canopy is struck by a blowpipe dart smeared with curare, it quickly loses its grip and falls to the ground.

It's a long way to Manaus, our next stop. Let's ride on one of the paddle steamers that have travelled the river for more than a hundred years.

4. The meeting of the waters

MANAUS IS THE BRAZILIAN CAPITAL of Amazonia. Near here, the Rio Solimões meets another great river - the Rio Negro, or 'black river'. The milky Solimões River is coloured by the silt carried from the slopes of the Andes, in Peru. But the Negro River is the colour of black tea. This river began in the lowland forests, and its colour comes from the litter of rotting plants. The two rivers flow side by side until the waters finally mix together. Then the river changes its name back to the Amazon for the last time.

Below: The Rio Negro and the Rio Solimões flow side by side for a while, after they meet in Brazil.

✋ PEOPLE *Floodplain communities*

People who live along this stretch of the river grow crops on the flat land on either side of the water. This land they use is called the várzea, or floodplain. In the wet season, the river spreads over the floodplain, depositing fertile silt. At this time of year, the várzea communities who live in stilt houses near the river have to move upstairs. For every várzea family, fish is an essential part of their diet. Children learn to fish almost before they can walk!

Above: Preparing manioc is a group effort. The process is a long one, and the whole community helps with each stage.

Right: Cabaclos people have learned that these palm berries make good wine. The people weave the palm leaves into baskets to carry the berries, and twist a strip of palm trunk into a handle.

💲 ECONOMY *Farming the floodplain*

When the water level recedes, people clear away the undergrowth and grow food on the fertilised land. Many families rely on the crops that they can grow themselves. The most important crop is manioc, a large root crop that grows well here. When the manioc tubers are big enough, farmers dig them up, peel them and boil them into a pulp. Then they squeeze out all the liquid, to get rid of juices that are poisonous. Once it has been dried in the sun, the manioc pulp is pounded into flour, which is called farinha.

✋ PEOPLE *Survival skills*

Many of the people who live in várzea communities have mixed ancestry. Their ancestors were AmerIndian, European and African. These people are called Caboclos, and they have retained many of the forest survival skills used by their AmerIndian ancestors.

Caboclos build temporary shelters in the forest. With strong beams and roofs made of palm fronds carefully woven together, these shelters can keep you dry during the heaviest rainstorm. Caboclos people spend the night here in hammocks suspended from hooks attached to the shelters' beams.

The rubber boom

About 150 years ago, people in Manaus struck gold! They discovered that a sticky liquid called latex, collected from rubber trees by AmerIndians, could make them rich. The invention of tyres in Europe meant that rubber was as valuable as gold. New types of steamboat could transport vast amounts of rubber down river. Then it could be exported to Europe. Manaus became a major port, and the population grew from 5,000 in 1865 to 50,000 by 1900.

The boom in rubber brought great wealth to Manaus. Rubber barons displayed their fortunes by building huge mansions and palaces. Manaus became the second city in Brazil to have electricity. The opera house, built in 1896, was a symbol of the new wealth and the city's international importance. This building is made of Scottish wrought iron and Italian stone. It is decorated with 36,000 French tiles, and has chandeliers made of Italian crystal and French bronze.

But by the early twentieth century, British traders had smuggled rubber seeds out of South America, and set up rival rubber plantations in south-east Asia. This new competition meant that the glory days of the rubber boom in Manaus were over.

Below: The beautiful coloured dome of the opera house in Manaus still stands out, and reminds you of the city's past. But now it is surrounded by the new giants - modern skyscrapers.

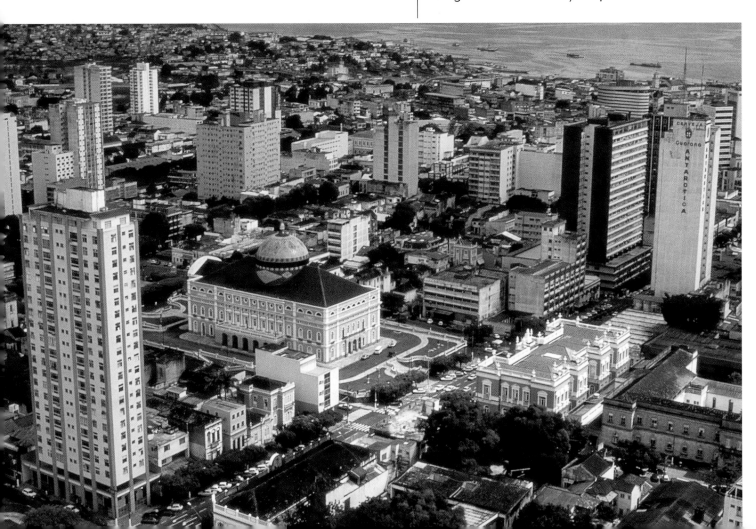

Above: These rubber tappers are members of a union and work together to protect their livelihood.
Right: This 'seringueiro' is making a diagonal cut into the bark of a rubber tree. Then he will attach a cup, to collect the latex that drips from the tree.

$ ECONOMY *Saving a way of life*

Today, the rubber boom is just a distant memory, but rubber tapping remains a way of life for many. Each rubber tapper, called a seringueiro, looks after about two hundred rubber trees. Every day, he takes a trail through the forest to set up the cups that will collect latex. On the return journey, the seringueiro takes a different trail, and picks up the latex from a previous trip. Back home, he heats the latex, and mixes it with vinegar to make it solid. He sells this to a rubber trader.

Chico Mendes will always be remembered by the seringueiros. Born into a rubber tapping family, Chico was a member of the rubber tappers' union, an organisation that protected the rights of the seringueiros. He saw that cattle ranchers and other landowners were taking over forest that was used by the seringueiros. Chico came up with the idea of setting up 'extractive reserves'. These are areas set aside for collecting latex and other natural products, without cutting down the trees. But the competition for land was fierce, and sometimes became violent.

In 1988, Chico was assassinated by one of his enemies. But Chico's 'extractive reserves' still safeguard the future of the seringueiros and the forest.

$ ECONOMY *A free trade zone*

Despite the slump in the rubber trade, Manaus has revived its fortunes. Now the city is an important industrial centre for four hundred electronics companies, because of its 'free trade zone'. This means that companies do not have to pay taxes on goods coming in and out of Manaus, which saves them a lot of money.

Companies can transport their products to and from Manaus airport, and then fly them all over the world. The port of Manaus can harbour ships that travel right down to the coast. This extra trade brings more money to the area, but it is not all good news. Some local people have lost their jobs, because modern electronics factories have replaced them with machines. The machines can produce goods even more cheaply.

Above: The port of Manaus has a special dock to handle dramatic changes in the water level of the Amazon River. Ships can travel here from the coast, which is 1,450 kilometres away.

➡ CHANGE *River power*

All these companies create a great demand for energy. The Amazon River is too slow and wide to be used to produce energy. But there are about eighty tributaries that feed into the Amazon. If these are dammed, hydroelectric power can be produced.

Some of the dams have not succeeded. Nearly thirty years ago, engineers began to build the Balbina Dam **MAP REF: 1** on the Uatumã River, near Manaus. The dam was finally finished in 1987, and the dam wall towered fifty metres, rising above the tops of the trees. But because the land is fairly flat, the river water has spread over a vast area behind the dam. It has flooded 236,000 hectares of forest.

Many local people think the Balbina Dam is a disaster. The Waimiri Artoari Indians who lived here were forced to leave their homes. They didn't receive compensation, nor have they benefited from the new source of electricity. And the dam's reservoir has become a swamp. Mosquitoes carrying diseases like malaria and yellow fever have multiplied. Plants have grown over the surface of the shallow, stagnant water.

Below: Behind the Balbina Dam, the drowned forest trees have been left to rot in the water. The reservoir is so shallow that some pieces of land break the surface of the water.

Weeds and dead leaves from the trees rot in the water, releasing millions of tonnes of methane and carbon dioxide. These gases pollute the atmosphere, and add to the problem of global warming.

The flat landscape creates another problem. There are no steep slopes, and so the water does not flow fast enough through the dam's turbines to generate power. The dam generates only a third of the energy originally estimated. This means the reservoir needs to flood an area the size of two football pitches to power just one air conditioner in downtown Manaus.

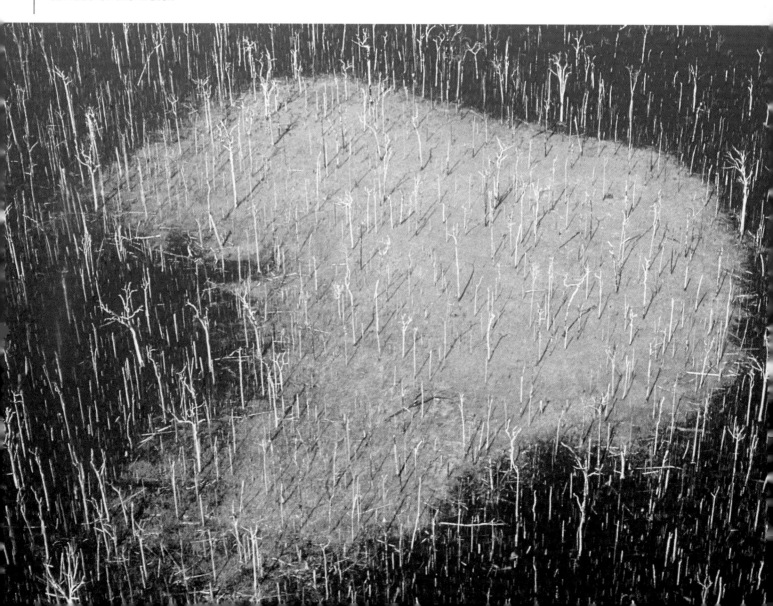

Adventure holiday

The city of Manaus is a growing centre for eco-tourism. This kind of tourism could help protect the traditional way of life, and the natural environment. Local people can benefit from eco-tourism. New jobs are created in hotels, lodges, restaurants and boats. There is an eco-tourism lodge on Silves Island MAP REF: 2 , 300 kilometres from Manaus. Some of the money made from visitors is used to protect the area's lakes, and create health services for local people. But eco-tourism has problems. By visiting remote areas, people still disturb the environment. Some eco-tourist attractions are foreign-owned, where local people share only a few of the benefits.

To reach Silves Island we travel to Itacoatiara, where the road ends. The rest of the five-hour journey is by voadeira - a canoe with a powerful engine. We may hear the call of a japin as we travel upriver. The japin bird copies the songs of other birds. It can even sound like a child crying.

We can try to catch piranhas in the flooded forest, with pieces of meat as bait. But piranha fishing is difficult for beginners. These fish can nibble away the meat at lightning speed.

Are you brave enough to go into the flooded forest at night? There are tarantulas, snakes, and caimans everywhere, and eyes glint red by flashlight all around us.

Left: This piranha fish will make a good lunch for visitors. AmerIndians don't just eat piranhas - they use the razor-sharp teeth as nail files, or to sharpen their weapons!
Below: By visiting hotels built among the trees of the forests, rich tourists can experience life in the Amazon, but still have luxury and comfort. This tower lookout helps tourists to spot forest birds.

Welcome to Ariaú Jungle Tower

Bem vindo ao Ariaú

✋ PEOPLE *A dance contest*

Tourists can enjoy the rich culture of the Manaus region in other places, too. There is a festival called Boi Bumbá, the Ox Dance, that is held on Parintins Island MAP REF: 3 , over a June weekend. This is the region's largest and most famous festival. The music and dance tells an ancient story of Catirina and her husband, Francisco. When she was pregnant, Catirina had a craving for ox-tongue. Francisco killed his master's best ox to keep her happy. But Francisco was thrown in prison for his crime. He was only freed when a man with magic powers, called Pajé, brought the ox back to life.

Each year, two dance and music troupes from Manaus compete in acting out the story. After three days of singing and dancing, the judges choose the winners. Winning first prize is a cause for great celebration, by both the dancers and their supporters.

Below: The Boi Bumbá, or Ox Dance, on Parintins Island.

We still have a long way to go before we reach the Atlantic Ocean. Let's buy a hammock in Manaus, so we can sleep on the ferry.

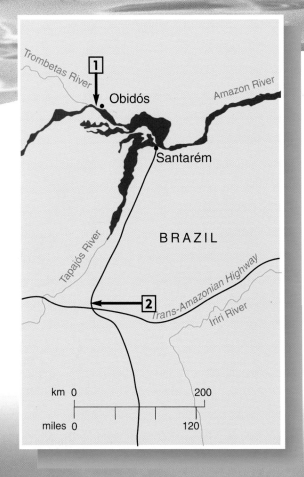

5. The Amazon floodplain

FROM MANAUS, WE CONTINUE TO TRAVEL EAST. The Amazon River is now muddy brown, coloured by all the silt it is carrying. After we reach the town of Santarém, we meet another tributary called the Tapajós River. This river flows up from the south. Its water is clear blue because - unlike the Amazon - it doesn't carry much silt with it.

Below: Sandbars like this one at Alter do Chão are made from silt that the river deposits as it slows down. Some sandbars get so high they could cut off parts of the river.

Above: The water of the Tapajós River is a clear blue. It joins the muddy Amazon near the town of Santarém.

🐇 NATURE The Óbidos Narrows

Forty million years ago, the movement of the Earth's plates pushed up an enormous inland sea between two mountain ranges, called the Guyanan Shield and the Brazilian Shield. The huge sea cut a deep channel between the mountains, as it began its journey to the Atlantic Ocean.

Today, this inland sea is part of the Amazon River. The channel that was cut between the two mountain ranges all those years ago is called the Óbidos Narrows MAP REF: 1. The river shrinks to a third of its width as it is forced through the Narrows, and that makes the water flow faster. This is the deepest and narrowest point on the Brazilian Amazon. The Óbidos Narrows form a natural gateway to the final stretch of the Amazon River's journey to the sea.

📖 HISTORY Guarding the fort

When the Portuguese controlled Brazil during the seventeenth century, they built a fort overlooking the river at Óbidos. Because the channel is so narrow, they could see across the river from the fort. They could keep watch for attacks from their enemies. During the early days of Portuguese rule, Óbidos was the largest town on this stretch of the river. Now the town is less important, but the old fort is a tourist attraction.

🐇 NATURE Tides & sediment

By this stage, the Amazon floodplain is vast. The river has deposited great mounds of sediment. The sediment makes sandy beaches on the inside bends of the river, where the current is weak. Beyond the river's banks, the land is flat as far as you can see. Much of this land is covered in water during the wet season, when the river bursts its banks. Even though we are still about 800 kilometres from the coast, the sea's tides can push water this far up the river.

Over thousands of years, some sea creatures like sting rays have moved with the tides, and now live here, far inland. Amazingly, they have been able to adapt successfully to the freshwater environment.

$ ECONOMY *Hidden treasure*

Beneath the rainforest along this stretch of the river, the land is rich in natural resources. There are plentiful supplies of important minerals such as copper, bauxite and manganese. And more than a million people have come to the Amazon basin in search of gold. Large swathes of forest have been turned into mud baths, where people dig, hoping to make their fortunes. Life as an Amazon gold-digger is very hard, however, and most people leave empty-handed.

NATURE *Searching for gold*

The Tapajós River valley is the largest gold mining region in the Amazon basin. Tiny specks of this precious metal can be found in the silt of the Tapajós River. Gold-diggers add liquid mercury to separate the gold from the

silt. But for every kilo of gold produced, four kilos of mercury is released into the environment. Some of the mercury escapes into the atmosphere as a poisonous gas, and more of it is washed into the soil or the river. Once the mercury is in the river, fish absorb it into their guts.

Mercury poisoning is very dangerous to humans. Too much mercury in your bloodstream causes tunnel vision, and alarming changes in behaviour. Acute poisoning can cause brain damage, and even death. People can be poisoned by breathing air polluted by mercury, or by eating fish full of mercury.

Thousands of people who live on the banks of the Tapajós River have mercury poisoning, because fish is the main item in their diet. In the gold mining town of Itaituba, along the Tapajós River, over a third of the miners have dangerously high levels of mercury in their blood.

➡️ **CHANGE** *Dredging the Tapajós*

There are plans to change the shape of the Tapajós River, by dredging a 1,000 kilometre section of the water. The dredged section will run upstream from Santarém, making the channel deeper and wider. If this happens, much bigger cargo ships will be able to take goods up the Tapajós River. Then they will be able to travel along the Amazon itself, all the way to the ocean.

Farmers who live far from the Amazon River are delighted by these plans. The wider channel will let them transport grains to markets in the United States and Europe. There, the grains are sold as cattle feed. But many local people are not so happy. Dredging will churn up silt and pollute the water. Waste from big cargo ships could make pollution even worse. Other people are worried about increased flooding in the wet season. The new channel will bring more water surging down the Tapajós River.

Left: More than one million miners, called garimpeiros, work in the goldfields of the Amazon River basin. They all hope to make their fortunes, but only a few will ever strike lucky.

$ ECONOMY *Opening the Amazon*

Since the 1970s, the Brazilian government has been encouraging people from overcrowded parts of Brazil to start a new life in the Amazon basin. Road-building has opened up areas, and linked river settlements to the outside world. The Trans-Amazonian highway runs for 5,000 kilometres across the region, and Santarém is connected to southern Brazil by a 1,741 kilometre road MAP REF: 2 . Other roads have been built illegally by logging companies. Tropical hardwoods, like mahogany, earn loggers a fortune in Japan, North America and rich European countries.

These roads act like magnets to new settlers. Families move in, and clear patches of forest to grow food. Other large areas are cleared by ranchers to make new pasture for raising cattle, or by companies growing crops in massive plantations.

A satellite image of the Amazon region, like the one on the opposite page, shows how much forest is being chopped down. Nearly 600,000 square kilometres of rainforest in Brazil has been destroyed since 1970. That area is the same size as the whole of France, or the whole of California.

Above: Cattle ranching is one of the most destructive uses of land. After only ten years, the land can look like a desert.

Now deforestation is speeding up. In 2000, nearly 20,000 square kilometres were destroyed. That's 6,000 square kilometres more than five years earlier.

Once the forest has gone, the soil quickly loses its fertility. Without the network of tree roots, nutrients are no longer recycled. Instead, they are easily washed away in a heavy rain shower, along with the soil. Some of this ends up in the river, adding to its already heavy load. With fewer trees, the nutrient supply to the river declines. That leaves less food for the Amazon's fish. And AmerIndian communities suffer, as their land is lost forever.

➡ CHANGE *Future frontiers*

Up to a quarter of the remaining rainforest in Brazil faces the chop over the next twenty years. More roads, dams and gas pipelines are all planned, as part of a project called 'Advance Brazil'. With this project, the Brazilian government hopes to open up more of the Amazon basin to farming, mining and logging.

Above: A satellite image of part of the Amazonian rain forest. The lighter areas show where the land has been cleared of trees.
Right: This close-up photograph shows the devastating effects of deforestation.

New jobs will be created, and the new industries can make money for the whole country. But 'Advance Brazil' is likely to cost as much as US$40 billion. Its effect on the rest of the rainforest may be disastrous.

We have nearly finished our journey. The final stage takes us across the delta to the river's mouth. There are hundreds of channels in the vast delta, so we must look for an experienced guide who knows the way!

6. Belém & the delta

ON THE LAST STRETCH OF OUR JOURNEY the Amazon River is very wide, and very deep. About 250 million litres of water drains from it, into the Atlantic Ocean, every second. Here, the river splits into a maze of channels, and dumps vast quantities of silt to form a delta. The islands of silt - like Marajó, the biggest - are home to many people. From Marajó, we will sail down the Pará River to the port of Belém. This is our final destination, close to the river's mouth.

Below: When the Amazon River gets close to the Atlantic Ocean it splits up into a maze of silty channels and islands.

Above: Pots from Marajó Island waiting to be shipped to other parts of Brazil for sale.
Right: Drums of different shapes and sizes are an important part of dances and festivals all over Brazil. Through the complex rhythms of the drum beat, many Brazilians celebrate their pride in their African heritage.

📖 HISTORY *Master potters*

Marajó MAP REF: 1 is one of the largest river islands in the world. It covers an area the size of Switzerland. Today, 250,000 people live there, but people have been living on Marajó for about two thousand years. Archaeologists have found pottery buried in the ground, that gives clues about life, all those years ago.

The Aruã Indians used to live on Marajó Island. The Aruã were one of the bravest Indian groups who fought the Portuguese, but they had disappeared entirely by the eighteenth century. The Aruã were masters of pottery.

Today, the way people make pots on Marajó is much the same as the Aruã before them. They take clay from the river bank, design and shape it into pots, and bake them hard in the sun before decorating them.

✋ PEOPLE *Songs of slavery*

Music and dancing on Marajó Island is also influenced by the past. Runaway African slaves found Marajó a good place to hide from their Portuguese masters. Some of those ex-slaves wrote the songs for a popular dance called the Carimbó. This is named after a tall drum, made from tree bark covered with deerskin on one end.

The Carimbó dance tells tales of sorrow. It recalls how the slaves missed their African homeland. But the dance is fun, too. Men and women dance to the rhythm of the drum in a big circle. When the women throw their handkerchiefs on the floor, their partners have to pick them up - but only with their mouths. That takes practice!

Left: The water around Marajó Island is stained brown with silt that has travelled with the river. Above: A family group of capybaras. They will dive under water at the first sign of danger.

also good swimmers, because of their three-toed webbed feet. But capybaras are endangered. Their habitat is shrinking, and people find them tasty to eat.

$ ECONOMY *Swimming buffalo*

Farmers have cleared many of the island's trees in the east of Marajó Island. This created large areas of grassland, called savanna. Here, some farmers grow rice, coconuts and a wide range of fruit and vegetables.

Other farmers rear large herds of cattle and water buffalo. According to local legend, water buffalo were introduced to Marajó a hundred years ago, when a ship was wrecked off the island's shores. These bulky animals cope well with Marajó's marshy, muddy grassland. They put their

NATURE *Giant rodents*

Marajó Island is just above sea-level. During the wet season in spring, parts of the island are submerged under water. Families of capybaras live in this soggy environment near the water's edge. Capybaras are the world's largest rodents. They are a bit like hamsters – but they can be one metre tall and weigh up to sixty kilograms! They are

Above: Water buffalo are good work animals. Their meat and hides are the main trade on Marajó Island.
Right: Coconut shells must dry in the sun before the outer fibre can be removed.

heads underwater to graze the flooded pasture, and don't mind swimming.

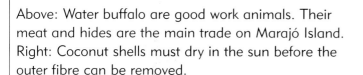 CHANGE *Coconut shell cars*

Nine hundred families who live on Marajó Island have found a way to make money from their plentiful supply of coconuts. Farmers sell fibres from coconut shells to a major car company. These hairy fibres are used in seats, head rests and sun visors of new cars that are sold in Brazil.

Through this new use of coconuts, farmers earn seven times more money than they used to. This new industry is good news for the environment, too. Unlike synthetic materials that are often used in car fittings, coconut fibres can be recycled. And if surplus coconut fibres are burned, they do not pollute the air like synthetics.

NATURE *Surfing the wave*

The ocean tides are very strong around the full moon in February and March, when spring tides pull the ocean water up the river channel. When the ocean whips back on the river, it makes a wave three metres high. Surfers arrive each year to surf the wave, called the pororoca. Some surfers can ride this wave for forty-five minutes!

HISTORY *Boom, bust & boom*

In 1616, the Portuguese established Belém as a port. From here they sent AmerIndian slaves, cocoa and spices from the Amazon basin to the outside world. Belém became the first base for Europeans along the Amazon. But fighting between Europeans and AmerIndians left many dead, and many AmerIndians were forced into slavery. The trade in slaves ended when slavery was finally abolished in Brazil in 1888.

Like Manaus upstream, Belém earned a new lease of life from rubber. It was brought here from all over the Amazon basin in the 1900s. Today Belém is the gateway to the world, for all the treasures of the Amazon. Nearly two million people now live here.

ECONOMY *Ver-O-Peso market*

From Belém, many timbers from the Amazon's forest begin their journey to market. Three-quarters of the timber is sold to Brazilians, but over twenty million cubic metres of timber are exported each year.

In the city, the Ver-O-Peso ('see the weight') market was originally a place for buying and selling slaves. Today, Ver-O-Peso is a market for anything that has been transported down the river. The fish hall displays fish for eating, and more exotic kinds that could end up in an aquarium. We could buy nuts, fruit and herbs, woven straw sieves, bottled snakes - even amulets to protect you from evil spirits.

ECONOMY *An Amazonian smoothie*

There is great excitement along Belém's waterfront when big boats loaded with açaí arrive. Açaí is a fruit of a palm tree that grows on the delta's river islands. People make a healthy fruit 'smoothie' by mixing açaí with manioc flour. Açaí ice cream is tasty too.

To collect açaí fruit, children climb the palm trees to reach the bunches of fruit at the top. Açaí growers harvest from the trees, rather than cutting them down. In this way the natural environment can remain intact, and future generations will still enjoy the taste of açaí.

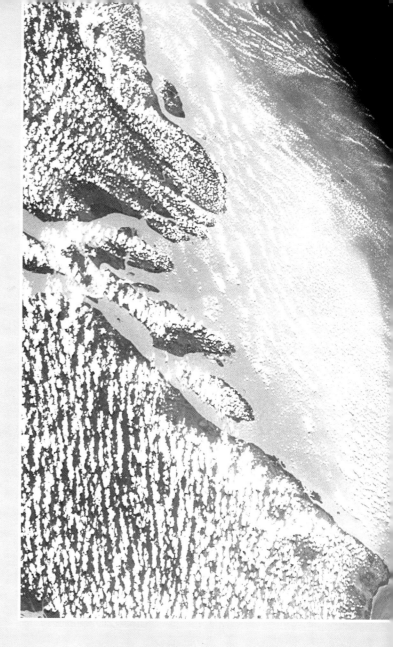

Above: Açaí fruit are off-loaded at the waterfront in Belém, ready for sale in the market.
Right: This satellite photograph shows the Amazon River meeting the Atlantic Ocean. You can see the plumes of silt spreading into the ocean.
Below: A load of timber is transported to market down the Amazon River.

At the end of our journey, the Amazon River is 240 kilometres wide. If we stand on one bank, it is impossible to see across this vast stretch of water to the other side. Every day, the river deposits over a million tons of silt into the ocean. Some of those particles of silt may have come with us on our journey, all the way from the Andes Mountains.

The Amazon falls 5,000 metres in the first 1,000 kilometres of its journey to the Atlantic Ocean.

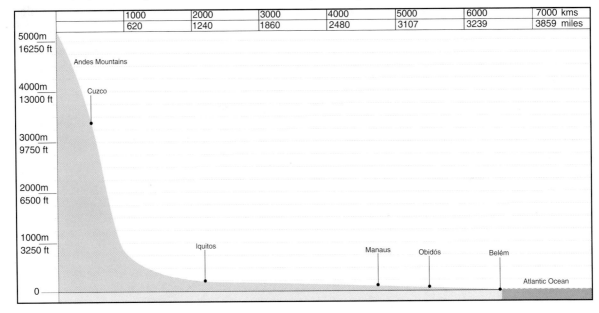

	1000	2000	3000	4000	5000	6000	7000 kms
	620	1240	1860	2480	3107	3239	3859 miles

Further Information

Useful websites

http://www.globaleye.org.uk/primary_autumn2001/focuson/index.html
A tour down the Amazon, illustrating some amazing facts.

http://www.geocities.com/CapitolHill/6502/amazon.html
Facts and photos about the Amazon river basin.

http://www.korubo.com/
An exploration to find an isolated Amazon tribe, the Tsohon-Djapa Indians. Includes a photo gallery.

http://www.amazonwatch.org/
Amazon Watch works with people in the Amazon basin to protect the environment and the rights of Amerindians.

http://www.pbs.org/journeyintoamazonia/
A well illustrated website that looks at different themes in the Amazon Basin.

http://www.pbs.org/wgbh/nova/shaman/
The Yanomami Indians and their way of life.

http://www.eduweb.com/amazon.html
Life in the Ecuadorian Amazon and the Quichua people who call it home. Includes games and on-line activities.

http://www.ran.org/info_center/index.html
The Rainforest Action Network website with lots of information and learning activities for schools.

Photographic sites

For satellite photos of the Amazon and its surrounding forest, go to http://www.grid.inpe.br/images.html

For photos of the upper parts of the Amazon river in Peru, go to www.amazon-ecotours.com/Photos.html

Or visit www.amazonthefilm.com which has photos, a quiz and part of a film about the Amazon river.

Books

We, the World A pack edited by Elizabeth Gilbert (Survival International 2000).

Our World: Living in the Rainforest by Terry Jennings (Channel Four 1998)

Focus on Rivers by Jane Featherstone (WWF-UK 2000)

Focus on the Aztecs and Incas by Chloe Sayer (Aladdin 1995)

People in the Rainforest by Saviour Pirotta (Wayland 1998).

Rainforest AmerIndians by Anna Lewington (Wayland 1992)

Trees and Plants in the Rainforest by Saviour Pirotta (Wayland 1998)

Glossary

Amulet   Something worn as protection against evil.

Architect   Someone who designs new buildings, parks and bridges.

Archaeologist   Someone who studies the remains of ancient civilisations.

Bank   The side of a river.

Bauxite   A mineral produced from weathered rock, used to make aluminium.

Canal   An artificial channel of water, cut for navigation or irrigation.

Catholicism   The beliefs and practices of the Catholic Church.

Cereal   Farm crops that produce grains such as wheat and maize.

Channel   The passage through which a river flows.

Cholera   A disease of the gut.

Confluence   The place where two rivers meet.

Current   The flow of water in a certain direction.

Dam   A barrier that holds or diverts water.

Decompose   To rot and break down.

Deforestation   The clearance of trees from land that was once covered by forest.

Delta   A geographical feature at the mouth of a river, formed by the build-up of sediment.

Descent   A downward change in height.

Diarrhoea   A bacterial infection of the gut.

Downstream   Towards the mouth of the river.

Drainage Basin   The area of land drained by a river and its tributaries.

Dredge   To clear or deepen a waterway or port, by scooping or sucking up sediment.

Floodplain   The flat part of a river valley that is submerged during floods.

Global warming   The gradual warming of the Earth's atmosphere as a result of greenhouse gases trapping heat. Human activity has increased the level of greenhouse gases, such as carbon dioxide and methane, in the atmosphere.

Gradient   The steepness of land, or the steepness of the fall of water. .

Habitat   The natural home of animals and plants.

Hydroelectric Power (H.E.P.)   Electricity generated by water as it passes through turbines.

Malaria   A disease carried by mosquitos.

Manganese   A hard, greyish white metal used to strengthen steel.

Mercury   A silvery white, poisonous metal.

Nomads   People who move around to find work or food or water.

Nutrients   Food. Plants use minerals as food.

Parasite   A living thing that feeds off another living thing, without helping its host in any way.

Plantation   A large farm.

Plate   Part of the Earth's crust.

Poacher   Someone who hunts or fishes illegally on someone else's land.

Predator   An animal that hunts and eats other animals.

Rapids   Fast-moving stretches of water.

Rio   The Portuguese and Spanish name for river.

Sap   Watery liquid that flows through a plant, carrying nutrients like sugars, salts and minerals.

Shaman   A priest who has special abilities to contact the spirit world.

Sonar   Sound waves that can travel underwater and spot any objects that may lie ahead.

Source   Where a river begins.

Tides   The rise and fall of an ocean's water as it is pulled by the moon and the sun.

Tributary   A stream or river that flows into a larger stream or river.

Tuber   The fleshy stem or root of a plant.

Tunnel Vision   A problem with eyesight, that means you can only see in front of you, and not the sides.

Upstream   Towards the source of the river.

Yellow Fever   A disease carried by mosquitos.

Index